Project Orangutan

Susan Ring

Weigl Publishers Inc.

Editor
Diana Marshall

Design and Layout
Warren Clark
Bryan Pezzi

Copy Editor
Jennifer Nault

Photo Researcher
Tina Schwartzenberger

Published by Weigl Publishers Inc.
123 South Broad Street, Box 227
Mankato, MN 56002 USA
Web site: www.weigl.com

Library of Congress Cataloging-in-Publication Data available upon request from the publisher.
Fax (507) 388-2746 for the attention of the Publishing Records Department.

ISBN 1-59036-058-3

Printed in the United States of America
1 2 3 4 5 6 7 8 9 0 06 05 04 03 02

DEVELOPED IN
COLLABORATION
WITH THE
MEMPHIS ZOO

Photograph Credits
Every reasonable effort has been made to trace ownership and to obtain permission to reprint
copyright material. The publishers would be pleased to have any errors or omissions brought
to their attention so that they may be corrected in subsequent printings.
Cover: baby orangutan (D. Robert Franz); **Ashley Averill/Memphis Zoo:** page 7; **Katrina
Burns/Memphis Zoo:** page 9; **Jennifer Coleman/Memphis Zoo:** page 4 right; **D. Robert Franz:**
pages 16, 17 far left, 17 left, 17 right, 17 far right, 20, 22 bottom; **Lisa Hailey/Memphis Zoo:** title
page; **Courtesy of the Houston Zoo:** page 13; **Michael Long/MaXx Images:** page 18; **Courtesy of
Memphis Zoo:** pages 3, 5, 8, 10, 14, 21 top right, 22 top; **Brian Parker/Tom Stack & Associates:**
pages 17 middle, 19; **Carrie Strehlau/Memphis Zoo:** pages 11, 12, 15, 21 left, 21 bottom right;
Doctor Chris Tabaka/Memphis Zoo: pages 4 left, 6; **Tom Stack & Associates:** page 23.

The Species Survival Plan® is a registered conservation program of the American Zoo &
Aquarium Association.

Contents

A Baby is Born

One day in November, a baby orangutan was born at the Memphis Zoo. The news pleased **zookeepers**. This rare treasure was the first orangutan born at the Memphis Zoo to survive in 15 years. He weighed 3.75 pounds at birth. That is about half the weight of a newborn human.

Zoo Issues

Should newborn baby animals be put on public display?

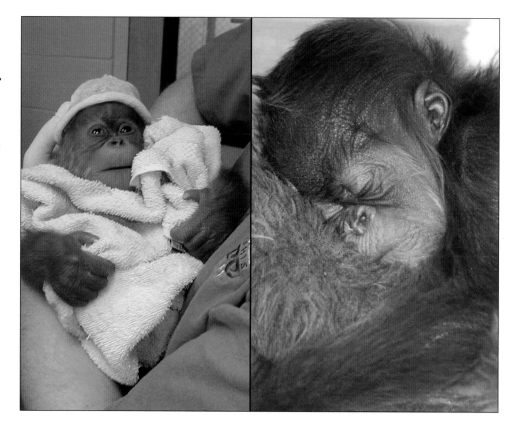

Like all newborn orangutans, the baby was covered in red fur. He did not have teeth, but his eyes were open.

The day the baby orangutan was born, zookeepers made a difficult decision. They knew that his mother had never taken care of a baby. They also observed some unhealthy reactions toward the newborn. They decided that it would be best for the baby to be raised by zoo staff.

The zoo **veterinarian**, Doctor Chris Tabaka, gave the baby a complete checkup. He looked for injuries and measured **hydration.** He made sure the newborn was healthy. A few months passed before the baby was ready to meet zoo visitors.

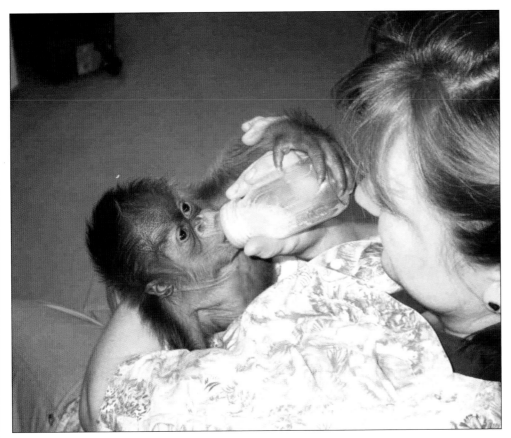

Every 2 hours, zookeepers fed the tiny orangutan from a bottle filled with special formula. They held him, rocked him to sleep, and burped him after meals.

Meet the Baby

One month after his birth, it was time to name the baby orangutan. The zookeepers picked five names. The zoo held a contest to choose one name. People who donated money to the zoo's **conservation** fund were given the chance to vote. The name Elok was chosen.

Zoo Issues

Think of some reasons why baby animals in zoos may need to be raised by humans.

Elok means "handsome" or "beautiful" in the Indonesian language.

BRAIN BOOSTERS

- In the wild, orangutans live in the **rain forests** of Borneo and Sumatra.

- There are two kinds of orangutans. They are the Bornean and the Sumatran. Elok is a Sumatran orangutan.

- Orangutans are the second largest of the apes. Gorillas are the largest.

- Baby orangutans drink their mother's milk until 3 to 4 years of age. During the next 3 to 5 years, they slowly become more independent.

- A mother orangutan pulls her baby on its belly around the nest. This helps the baby learn to crawl. She tickles and plays with her baby. This keeps the baby active and happy.

Holding on to Doctor Chris Tabaka made Elok feel safe and secure.

At first, Elok could not focus his eyes or crawl. Orangutans are helpless for the first few weeks of life. Still, he had a very strong grip. Orangutans are born with the **instinct** to hang on to their mothers. Elok held on to the zookeepers the same way he would have clung to his mother's fur. He did not like being far from them. He would scream and cry when he had to let go. Working in shifts, zookeepers cared for him day and night. They fed him, cleaned him, and kept him warm. Elok was never alone.

Elok Explores

When Elok turned 4 months old, he spent 7 hours each day in a nursery that was on public display. Visitors watched him play with sticks, hay, **bamboo,** and baby toys. He built strength, speed, and coordination. Some evenings, he played outside in the adult orangutans' yard. He learned about water by watching the waterfall and feeling its spray. For safety reasons, adult orangutans were not allowed in the yard while Elok was outside.

Zoo Issues

Why is it important for zoo food to be similar to animals' food in the wild?

Elok was very curious. He explored the stream and played in the tall, green grass.

Playing in the outside yard taught Elok about flowers, birds, squirrels, and rain.

BRAIN BOOSTERS

- During their first 2 years of life, orangutans' rate of development is similar to that of human babies.

- Young orangutans nap in leafy nests they make themselves in trees.

- At 4 to 5 months of age, baby orangutans in the wild try eating adult food. They do this by taking food out of their mother's mouth.

- Orangutans live with their mother until they are about 8 years old.

- Orangutans eat fruit, such as mangoes, figs, and bananas. These fruits grow in rain forests. They also eat birds' eggs, ants, and termites.

Elok adjusted well to change. He was brave and learned to play by himself. Soon, he was crawling and playing on the nursery floor. When Elok was 5 months old, zookeepers set broom handles between two chairs. This was Elok's first chance to climb and swing. One month later, he could climb and swing on ropes in the nursery. This was like playing in trees in a rain forest. Elok learned many games. He loved to climb a rope into a basket. He also learned to play tricks on the zookeepers. Often, he would grab their papers when they were not looking.

Meet the Parents

Like Elok, Puti was raised by humans.

Elok's mother is a smart orangutan named Puti. She loves to take things apart. She was born in 1981. Puti was 19 years old when she gave birth to Elok. The baby's father was born in 1982. His name is Tombak. Puti and Tombak came to the Memphis Zoo together in 1994, from Atlanta, Georgia.

Zoo Issues

Should breeding in zoos be controlled and monitored?

While at the Memphis Zoo, Puti and Tombak have always lived together. They liked each other from the start. Right before Elok was born, Puti and Tombak were separated for a short time. Puti stayed inside. She was kept away from the zoo visitors and the outside yard. This allowed her to give birth to her baby in a quiet, safe place. Now, Puti and Tombak are together in the orangutan **exhibit** during the day. At night, they are separated because Puti is on a special diet.

When Tombak became an adult, he developed large cheek pads and throat pouches.

A New Family for Elok

In the wild, male orangutans do not help raise babies. Adult orangutans do not live together the way some other apes do. Mother orangutans take care of the young alone. Puti had never been around baby orangutans before Elok was born. She did not know how to care for him. The zookeepers saw signs that Puti was not ready to properly care for a baby. That is why they took care of Elok from the start.

Zoo Issues

Think of some reasons why zoo animals may need to be separated.

When Elok turned 1 year old, the zoo held a big birthday party for him.

Cheyenne loves Elok. She treats him as if he was her own baby.

Brain Boosters

- Female orangutans are fully grown by 9 or 10 years of age. They are able to have babies at this time.

- Adult female orangutans weigh between 80 to 100 pounds. Adult male orangutans weigh between 150 and 250 pounds.

- Puti and Tombak are very smart. They have learned to show zookeepers their head, shoulders, back, teeth, and other body parts.

Soon after his first birthday, zookeepers chose a new home for Elok. He was adopted by an orangutan named Cheyenne at the Houston Zoo. Cheyenne had already been a caring mother to another baby she adopted, named Luna. By this time, Elok had met other orangutans. He was not afraid of the change. Right away, Cheyenne took excellent care of him.

The Zoo Crew

The baby orangutan needed constant care.

Zookeepers are important to all zoo animals. For Elok, the zookeepers at the Memphis Zoo were extra special. Without them, he could not have grown into a healthy orangutan. The zookeepers did not just feed him and clean his exhibit. They took turns spending time with him 24 hours a day.

Doctor Tabaka kept Elok healthy. He gave Elok **vaccines**, medicines, and other things babies need to stay well.

The people who built the orangutan exhibit are also important. They made the orangutans' zoo home feel like their natural **habitat**.

Elok was given toys that would help him learn, grow strong, and stay active.

HOW CAN I BECOME A NURSERY KEEPER?

A nursery keeper feeds and takes care of zoo babies whose mothers are unable to care for them. Nursing experience or a degree is helpful. A strong desire to care for baby animals is a must. Animal training can be gained by volunteering at local zoos or veterinary clinics.

ZOO RULES

The orangutans are not bothered by visitors. Often, Elok tried to touch the people he saw through the glass. He was interested in funny hats and bright-colored clothes. It is a treat to see rare, wild animals up close. That is why it is important to respect the zoo and the animals. Zoos have rules that help keep animals and visitors safe and healthy.

Memphis Zoo's Rules:
1. Do not tap on the glass.
2. Let the animals sleep.
3. Do not take pictures with a flash.
4. Stay behind the railing.
5. Do not throw anything into the yard.

Animal Gear

When is a foot like a hand? When it belongs to an orangutan. Along with their feet and hands, many features set orangutans apart from other animals. Another unusual feature is the stringy, red fur that covers their bodies.

Zoo Issues

Why should zoo exhibits be similar to an animal's natural habitat?

Thumbs

Orangutans are part of a group of animals called **primates**. All primates have feet and hands that can grasp things using their thumbs. Thumbs help them hold on to sticks, leaves, and fruit. Thumbs also help them swing from tree branch to tree branch.

Arms and Legs

The body of an orangutan is made to swing. Their arms are almost twice as long as their legs. When they stand, their strong arms almost reach down to their ankles. A mother will stretch out between two trees. She acts like a bridge for her babies.

Cheeks and Throat

Large cheek pads on an adult male orangutan's face make it look larger than it really is. This may help scare away **predators**. Drooping throat pouches help male orangutans make very loud, groaning, bubbling sounds. These can be heard almost 1 mile away.

Eyes

Like all primates, orangutans' eyes face forward. This helps them judge how far away objects are. Unlike most animals, the white part of their eyes is visible. Their eyes show all kinds of feelings, from thoughtful to afraid, and from sad to angry.

Teeth

While they use their teeth to chew food, orangutans may also use them to communicate. By showing their teeth, they can express feelings, such as sadness and happiness. Their strong jaws and teeth are used to crack nuts, grind bark, and open fruit.

In the Wild

Male orangutans live alone. They come near female orangutans only to mate. The males try to avoid each other. They stay in their own **territories**. At least once each day, male orangutans let other males know where they are. They do this very loudly. They break off a tree branch, which they bang on the ground. Then, they make a long call, using their throat pouches. The call gets louder and louder.

Orangutans are the largest primates that live in trees.

Adult orangutans spend most of their time gathering food to eat. Female orangutans keep watch over their babies. When two orangutan families meet in the wild, the young enjoy playing together. They climb trees, swing on vines, and run along the forest floor.

Orangutans spend most of their lives in treetops. Baby orangutans hang on to their mother while she swings from branch to branch.

Tree Territory

The rain forests of Borneo and Sumatra that orangutans call home are being cut down. Every day, orangutans lose more of their habitat. As a result, the world's wild orangutan population is quickly disappearing. In 1993, about 12,000 orangutans lived in the wild. By 2002, this number had decreased to 4,000.

Zoo Issues

How can zoos help wild animal populations?

Orangutans are losing the trees they need to find fruit and make nests.

- Sumatran orangutans, like Elok, are the most endangered orangutans.

- Orangutans are very smart. In zoos, orangutans have learned to tie knots, choose the right key for a lock, and use sign language.

- People can learn about orangutans by watching them in zoos. The more people know about orangutans, the better the animals' chance of survival will be in the wild. Research can help breeding decisions. Some zoo orangutans can even be reintroduced into the wild.

Each new baby orangutan born in a zoo strengthens the wild orangutan population.

Many orangutans are **smuggled** out of their country. They are sold to people as pets. They are sent on ships to other countries. Many do not survive this long journey.

The good news is that conservation workers are helping these orangutans. They rescue young orangutans and take them back to the rain forests. By **reintroducing** the orangutans to their natural habitats, conservation workers help the animals learn to survive in the wild.

Orangutan Issues

Benefits of Zoo Life

- No danger from predators, hunting, competition, or habitat loss
- Regular food, play time, and medical care
- Can help educate the public about orangutans
- Can be reintroduced into wild orangutan populations
- Is easier to research orangutans in zoos
- Can live a longer life

Benefits of Life in the Wild

- More natural space in which to feed and live
- Maintain diverse orangutan populations
- Daily mental and physical challenges, such as finding food
- Part of the natural web of life consisting of plants, predators, and prey
- Live complex lives
- Maintain independence

Folk Tale

From Human to Orangutan

One legend from Southeast Asia describes the similarity between orangutans and humans. The story explains that bird gods created men and women. The bird gods were so happy with their creations that they held a big celebration. The feast lasted many days. When it was over, the bird gods tried to create more people. Unfortunately, they had forgotten how to create people. Instead, they accidentally created the orangutan.

Source: McDearman, Kay, *Orangutans*. New York: A Skylight Book, 1983.

More Information

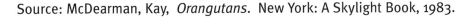

The Internet can lead you to some exciting information on orangutans. Try searching on your own, or visit the following Web sites:

American Zoo and Aquarium Association (AZA)
www.aza.org

Memphis Zoo www.memphiszoo.org

National Geographic Kids
www.nationalgeographic.com/kids/creature_feature/
0102/orangutans.html

Sumatran Orangutan Society www.orangutans-sos.org

CONSERVATION GROUPS

There are many organizations involved in orangutan research and conservation. You can get information on orangutans by writing to the following addresses:

INTERNATIONAL
World Wildlife Fund
International
Avenue du Mont-Blanc
CH-1196, Gland
Switzerland

UNITED STATES
Orangutan Foundation
International
822 South Wellesley Avenue
Los Angeles, CA
90049-9963

Words to Know

bamboo: tall, stiff grass that grows in Asia

breeding program: producing babies by mating selected animals

conservation: the care and monitoring of animals and animal populations for their continued existence

endangered: animals whose numbers are so low that they are at risk of disappearing from the wild

exhibit: a space on display that looks similar to an animal's natural habitat

gestation period: the time from the beginning of pregnancy to the birth

grooming: cleaning by plucking bugs, dirt, and other things out of the fur

habitat: place in the wild where an animal naturally lives

hydration: water levels in the body

instinct: something an animal knows naturally, without being taught

predators: animals that hunt and kill other animals for food

primates: animals that have large brains and can grab things with their fingers or toes, especially using their thumbs

rain forests: dense woodlands that get large amounts of rain

reintroducing: putting an animal or population back into a habitat

smuggled: carried out of a country illegally

solitary: living alone

territories: areas that an animal will defend as its own

vaccines: medicines to prevent sickness

veterinarian: animal doctor

zookeepers: people at a zoo who feed and take care of the animals

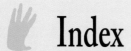 # Index